ENGINEERING
in Your Everyday Life

Enslow Publishing
101 W. 23rd Street
Suite 240
New York, NY 10011
USA
enslow.com

Danell Dykstra

REAL WORLD SCIENCE

Published in 2020 by Enslow Publishing, LLC
101 W. 23rd Street, Suite 240, New York, NY 10011

Copyright © 2020 by Enslow Publishing, LLC.

All rights reserved.

No part of this book may be reproduced by any means without the written permission of the publisher.

Library of Congress Cataloging-in-Publication Data

Names: Dykstra, Danell, author.
Title: Engineering in your everyday life / Danell Dykstra.
Description: New York : Enslow Publishing, 2020. | Series: Real world science | Audience: Grades 5-8. | Includes bibliographical references and index.
Identifiers: LCCN 2018050180| ISBN 9781978507623 (library bound) | ISBN 9781978509511 (paperback)
Subjects: LCSH: Engineering–Juvenile literature.
Classification: LCC TA149 .D95 2020 | DDC 620–dc23
LC record available at https://lccn.loc.gov/2018050180

Printed in the United States of America

To Our Readers: We have done our best to make sure all website addresses in this book were active and appropriate when we went to press. However, the author and the publisher have no control over and assume no liability for the material available on those websites or on any websites they may link to. Any comments or suggestions can be sent by email to customerservice@enslow.com.

Photo Credits: Cover, p. 1 Veres Production/Shutterstock.com; cover, p. 1 (science icons), back cover pattern kotoffei/Shutterstock.com; cover, p. 1 (globe graphic) Elkersh/Shutterstock.com; cover, interior pages (circular pattern) John_Dakapu/Shutterstock.com; p. 5 Reinnier Kaze/AFP/Getty Images; p. 9 A7880S/Shutterstock.com; p. 11 Vitalliy/Shutterstock.com; pp. 13, 21, 34, 41, 47 Danell Dykstra; p. 16 Sunny MeansSixteen/Shutterstock.com; p. 19 © iStockphoto.com/KaraGrubis; p. 24 Nasky/Shutterstock.com; p. 25 Kitch Bain/Shutterstock.com; p. 27 Sergey Merkulov/Shutterstock.com; p. 31 udaix/Shutterstock.com; p. 32 J. Lekavicius/Shutterstock.com; p. 37 rjmiguel/Shutterstock.com; p. 39 1989studio/Shutterstock.com; p. 45 Jenson/Shutterstock.com; p. 53 Kekyalyaynen/Shutterstock.com; p. 54 manfredxy/Shutterstock.com.

Contents

Introduction 4

■ **Chapter 1**
Bridges 8

■ **Chapter 2**
Plastics 15

■ **Chapter 3**
Batteries 23

■ **Chapter 4**
Cars 29

■ **Chapter 5**
Smartphones 36

■ **Chapter 6**
Robots 43

■ **Chapter 7**
Water 50

Chapter Notes 57
Glossary 61
Further Reading 62
Index 63

Introduction

Cars, phones, bridges, and batteries are all built based on designs developed by engineers. Solving a problem, building a gadget, and meeting requirements are all part of everyday engineering. Ever experienced an electrical power outage and realized how many things needed electricity? You will be surprised to learn just how many things need engineering.

Simple experiments will allow you to explore several areas of engineering, including mechanical engineering with cars, civil engineering with bridges, and environmental engineering with water. Enjoy your new insight into the engineering behind everyday objects that make your life simpler, such as smartphones and batteries. Puzzle over the impact you could have on your environment with a simple faucet aerator that saves gallons of water. Imagine the developments happening today in our ever-changing world and how you will someday take part in that technology development.

In the future, you may start a career in science, technology, engineering, or math (STEM). If you find engineering interesting, start in high school by taking challenging classes, such as calculus and physics. In the first year of college, an engineering major usually takes an introductory engineering course plus calculus, physics, and sometimes chemistry. Engineering offers a broad range of interesting study possibilities and career opportunities. Some people prefer indoor computer programming and others prefer outdoor construction. Some people focus on community work while others enjoy traveling internationally. Some individuals

Introduction

A mechanical engineer in Cameroon, a nation in Africa, works on a drone. Engineering design teams create new devices to meet a specific need or request. Often the concept is drawn on computer software before the model is built and tested.

Engineering in Your Everyday Life

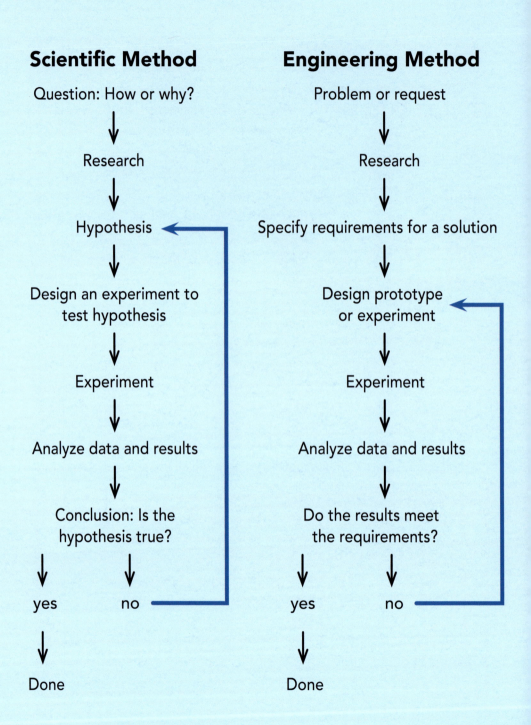

Introduction

are comfortable in predictable low-risk applications while others seek out cutting-edge, creative, high-risk development.

Creativity is important in the engineering method, which is different from the scientific method. The scientific method steps include asking a question, making a hypothesis, and testing. Scientists study how science works. Engineers are scientists, but they also design new devices, novel software, and innovative solutions. Engineers start with a problem and work to meet a set of requirements. The requirements include asking who has this problem, what exactly is the problem, and why do they need a solution. For example, a client requests a machine that will fly a camera over the house to inspect roof damage; engineers develop drones.

Notice that on the engineering method on the right column, it loops back to designing a prototype or experiment. Engineers learn with each test and take that new insight and adjust the design to test again. If an experiment does not "work" or meet the requirements, take the results, modify the design, and experiment again, similar to every engineer.[1]

Performing experiments is a good way to get a feel for engineering design. Follow the detailed steps provided for each activity. Be creative but always remember safety. It is important to keep safe:
- **Protect yourself from splashes with goggles, protective clothing, and closed-toe shoes.**
- **If you have long hair, tie it back.**
- **Wash your hands when you finish.**
- **Do not eat or drink while experimenting.**

Bridges

Bridges span rivers, roads, railroad tracks, and valleys. They are made of strong materials such as stone, concrete, or steel, but they are also based on smart designs. Civil engineers design bridges, roads, and even skyscrapers.

A bridge designed for people to walk over does not need to be as strong as a bridge for heavy cars and trucks. How strong does a bridge have to be? Gravity is the pulling force that makes stuff fall to the ground. Weight is the mass times the gravitational pull. A bridge is designed for the weight of the bridge plus the maximum weight of the objects that cross the bridge, such as people, cars, and even massive trains. Engineers carefully calculate the worst case and then add a safety factor to make the bridge extra strong. Why is this important? If not designed correctly, a bridge could collapse!

There are four basic bridge types: beam, truss, arch, and suspension.[1]

Beam Bridges

The simplest bridge is a beam bridge. If you ever put a wood plank or log across a stream, then you have built a beam bridge. Standing on a bridge, your weight is a downward force. Based on Newton's third law, for every force, there is an equal and opposite force. The supports on each end of the bridge make an equal opposite force, pushing up. The net force is zero. If the force of the weight exceeds the bending moment of the bridge—think stiffness—the beam bridge will bend until it snaps, breaks, and collapses!

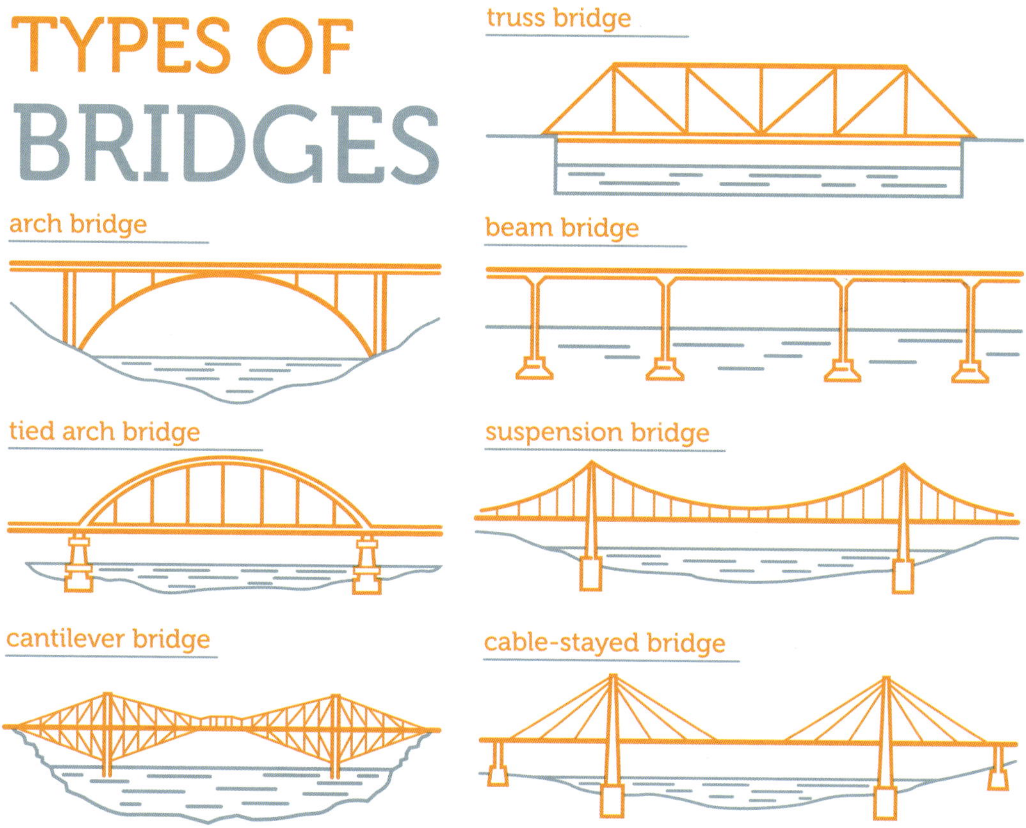

Bridges

TYPES OF BRIDGES

- arch bridge
- truss bridge
- beam bridge
- tied arch bridge
- suspension bridge
- cantilever bridge
- cable-stayed bridge

Many bridges combine beam, truss, arch, and suspension. The tied arch bridge uses the tension cables of a suspension bridge. Find the beam and truss in the cantilever bridge.

Truss Bridges

Sometimes, based on heavy loads, engineers select a truss bridge design. Notice the triangles in a truss bridge. The truss bridges can carry amazing loads, such as trains. The triangle design is sturdy, with each triangle distributing a force, either compression or

Engineering in Your Everyday Life

tension. Compression is a pushing force, similar to chewing gum. Tension is a pulling force, like a rope tug-of-war. In a truss bridge, some parts are in compression, while others balance in equal tension. The triangles allow the truss bridge to carry heavy loads.

All around you are things using this same triangle principle for stiffness. Look closely at the end of corrugated cardboard. A wavy piece of paper is sandwiched between two other pieces of paper, acting like a truss. Each of the center paper waves in cardboard helps strengthen the cardboard.

Arch Bridges

In ancient times, the Romans built stone arch bridges that are still standing.[2] The force on an arch bridge travels down the sides to the bases, which are called abutments. Rocks or stones work well in this compressive force. To build a stone arch bridge, a half circle brace is built and then starting at the abutment, each stone is placed on top of the other from the bottom up on both sides. The last stone to be put in place, at the very top of the arch, is called the keystone. Then the half circle brace is removed. Today, arch bridges are usually built with concrete and steel.

Suspension Bridges

The Golden Gate Bridge and Brooklyn Bridge are extraordinary suspension bridges. Cables and towers suspend the road. This is an elegant solution to a very long bridge requirement. Like a swing on a swing set, the cables are in tension. Each cable supports a small fraction of the total bridge weight. If a bridge has one hundred vertical cables, then each can support $1/100^{th}$ of the total weight. The force of the cables is in tension, and the towers are in compression. If a bridge has more cables, do they each carry more or less weight?

Ferris Wheels

Chicago was chosen to hold the 1893 World's Fair. The city wanted to build something to rival Paris's Eiffel Tower from the previous World's Fair. George Ferris (1859–1896) was building bridges with a new, strong metal—steel. Ferris, a civil engineer, proposed a brilliant idea. Why not build a wheel ride with steel instead of wood? A steel wheel could be so much taller. Ferris built his 250-foot (76-meter) wheel. It carried more than two thousand passengers at a time, high above the fairgrounds. It has been called a Ferris wheel ever since. Can you find the truss (triangle) design in the wheel support?[3]

The truss bridge principle is used to design a Ferris wheel; the spokes (white structures) hold the wheel in tension.

Engineering in Your Everyday Life

Factors to Consider

Engineers have to research local weather history before building a bridge. What are the highest winds, coldest and warmest temperatures, and even the risk of an earthquake? In 1940, engineers learned about a complex phenomena where light winds caused the flutter effect on a bridge. The Tacoma Narrows Gallopin' Gertie swung, twisted, and turned in the breeze until it crumbled into the water below.[4]

Activity: Test Bridge Designs

Your challenge is to build a model bridge that can support one hundred pennies using paper as the building material.

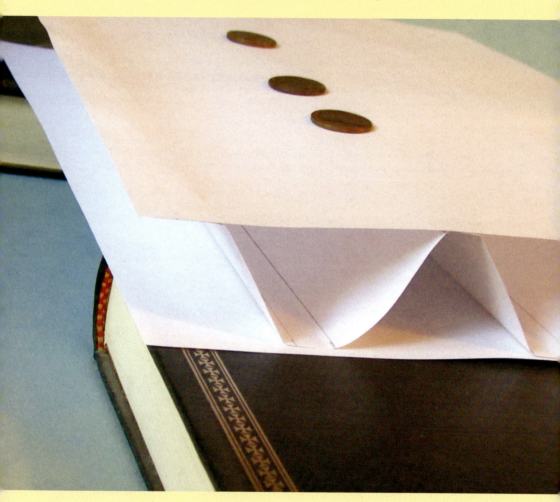

Build a truss bridge with a folded sheet glued between a top and bottom sheet. Set the bridge across two books. Test the strength by adding pennies until failure.

Engineering in Your Everyday Life

Things You Will Need:

- 10 pieces of printer paper
- a glue stick
- a pencil
- a ruler
- 2 books of similar thickness
- 100 pennies

■ **1.** First build your bridges before testing.

■ **2.** Plywood is thin wood layers glued together for increased strength. Like plywood, glue together three pieces of paper to make a three-layer beam bridge.

■ **3.** To make a six-layer beam bridge, fold three pieces of paper lengthwise. Glue each fold closed, and then glue all three together.

■ **4.** To build a truss bridge, draw lines across the length of the paper alternating between a ½-inch (1-centimeter) width and a 1½-inch (4-cm) width. Then fold on each line to make it accordion style, forming M shapes.

■ **5.** Use the glue stick along each of the ½-inch folds to glue a piece of paper on top and another on the bottom.

■ **6.** When the glue has dried, test the bridges. Set two books of similar thickness on a table with 7½ inches (19 centimeters) between them. Lay a single piece of paper so that each end is on a book. Does it support a penny? Now test each bridge by adding one penny at a time until the bridge fails. Is the six-layer bridge stiffer than the three-layer bridge? Can the truss bridge support a hundred pennies?

Plastics

Chapter 2

How many times a day do you use plastics? Check the tags of your clothes, because polyester clothes are woven with plastic fibers. Does the trash can have a bag liner? What about a smartphone case? Did you drink from a plastic bottle? Plastics can be clear or colored, lightweight, molded into many shapes, and very cheap.

Chemical Composition

What is a plastic anyway? At the chemical level, plastics are primarily made of carbon and hydrogen molecules. Like building blocks in a long chain, carbon and hydrogen molecules bond in repeating patterns. To form plastic, five hundred to twenty thousand or more of these repeating patterns can link together. Oil and natural gas provide the building blocks of carbon and hydrogen to make intermediates, for example, ethylene (C_2H_4). Polymerization of ethylene converts it to polyethylene.[1]

Manufacturing Plastics

Chemical engineers design facilities that convert oil and natural gas into ethylene and propylene, and then to polyethylene and polypropylene. Fascinating complex problems are given to engineers to design, operate, and optimize a facility. Those chemical plants compress gas, heat the feed, control the chemical reaction, and separate the products.

One product is the small plastic resin pellet, polyethylene, which is about the size of a green pea.[2] At the plastics manufacturing

Engineering in Your Everyday Life

plant, the pellets are heated to their melting point. The melted pellets become a hot, soft, viscous material like slime. Next, it is blown into a mold. It cools and hardens in the mold. When cooled, it is removed from the mold and it keeps its shape.[3] Now you have a bottle, cup, or bag. Plastic is used for many products because it is lightweight, inexpensive, and can be made into so many shapes and products. You will witness firsthand plastic cooling and hardening in the next activity.

Polyethylene pellets can be easily transported to a variety of manufacturing plants where they are melted and formed into products, such as grocery bags.

Plastics

3D Printing

A 3D printer converts a digital computer concept model into a three-dimensional object by "printing" one thin layer on top of another layer. This process is also called additive manufacturing. Plastic is melted around 400°F (200°C), extruded to a very thin string, and laid down in a film on top of film to make a three-dimensional product.[4] The hot plastic fuses to the layer above and below it, before it cools and hardens—like a hot glue gun. These printers can be used to make more than just plastic products—they can even be used for making chocolate and jewelry![5]

As kids, your great-grandparents may not have used plastic forks or spoons. Plastics did not become common for packaging until the late 1940s. Engineers innovated and developed plastic tape, plastic wrap for food, plastic storage containers, spray bottles, garbage bags, and zipper storage bags.[6] People bought the plastic products because they were cheap, lightweight, and disposable.

Recycling Plastics

Plastic is great to use, but in a landfill it can take up to one thousand years to decompose.[7] Paper, glass, and aluminum can be recycled, but there are many different kinds of plastics.

Why do the various types of plastics have to be separated before recycling? For starters, they are used for different products. But they also have different melting point temperatures. The

Engineering in Your Everyday Life

melting point of a water bottle (PET) is close to 500°F (260°C), but plastic wrap (LDPE) is almost half that at 356°F (180°C).[8] A plastic recycling revolution started in 1988 when the Society of the Plastics Industry established a coding system for plastics.[9] Pick up a plastic bottle and read the recycle triangle number on the bottom. Check the chart below to find out what kind of plastic you are holding.[10]

SPI Coding System

Recycle Number	Acronym	Chemical Name	Common Example
1	PET	Polyethylene terephthalate	Water bottles
2	HDPE	High-density polyethylene	Milk jugs
3	V	Polyvinyl chloride	Credit cards
4	LDPE	Low-density polyethylene	Plastic wrap
5	PP	Polypropylene	Clear plastic bags
6	PS	Polystyrene	Plastic forks and spoons
7	Other		Nylon fabrics

Plastics

Throughout your day, you will come across many different plastic products. This triangle stamped into playground equipment is recycle number 2, high-density polyethylene, the same material as milk jugs.

At the recycling facility, plastics ride a conveyor belt for sorting.[11] After sorting, sharp blades chop the plastic into little pieces. Next, the plastic pieces are washed with detergent and water to remove food and labels. Then the recycled pieces are melted, extruded (think of spaghetti noodles), and cut into pellets.[12]

Engineering in Your Everyday Life

Bioplastics

Recycling plastics is much better for the environment than putting plastics in a landfill, but all the same, when the plastics are made, pollutants are produced. Another concern is that someday the oil and gas will run out—some say in the next one hundred years.[13] Therefore, scientists and engineers are working together for other solutions. One idea is biodegradable plastics. Two great things about biodegradable plastics are that they are made from a renewable resource (plants) and they can decompose faster, like in your lifetime. Bioplastics use the plant starch as a polymer. When heated, the starch bonds break, leaving sites for the hydrogen in water to bond. Glycerol acts as a plasticizer between the starch polymers.[14] The reason scientists and engineers are working on this problem is because bioplastics have different properties than oil- and gas-based plastics. Remember how engineers work to meet requirements? There is still design work happening. Two bioplastics being made today are corn based polylactide acid (PLA) and polyhydroxyalkanoate (PHA).[15]

Activity: Make Biodegradable Plastics

Make and compare two bioplastics! For the first version, use cornstarch like PLA as the source of carbon. In the second bioplastic, use gelatin as the carbon source. Like an engineer, compare the properties and possible applications of the two bioplastics. For safety, have an adult help you with this activity, which involves a hot stovetop and boiling.

The cornstarch plastic has blue food coloring, while the gelatin plastic has green food coloring to help distinguish the two products.

Engineering in Your Everyday Life

Things You Will Need:

- ½ cup (100 ml) water
- 1 tbsp (15 mL) glycerin (sometimes also called glycerol, available in some drugstores)
- 1 tbsp (15 mL) cornstarch
- 3 packages of gelatin (21g).
- 2 tsp (10 mL) vinegar
- 2 drops of food coloring (optional, you may use a different color for each bioplastic)
- a saucepan
- a whisk
- a spatula
- aluminum foil

■ **1.** Pour all the ingredients EXCEPT the gelatin into a saucepan. Mix with a whisk until the lumps are gone.

■ **2.** Place the saucepan on the stove. Turn the heat to medium high. Stir continuously with the spatula. In five to ten minutes, it will turn from opaque to translucent. The chemical reaction is complete when it gently boils and thickens.

■ **3.** Remove from the heat.

■ **4.** Put a piece of aluminum foil on a flat surface. Carefully pour the hot plastic out of the pan onto the aluminum foil. Allow the plastic to dry for two days. The plastic will dry faster if it is thinner.

■ **5.** Try this procedure again, but replace the cornstarch with three packages of gelatin. How do the two plastics compare after drying? Is one more flexible than the other?

Batteries

Chapter 3

Can you imagine your life without batteries? Smartphones would be plugged in. The TV remote would have to be plugged in. An electric car with a very long electrical extension cord would not be practical. Batteries are so common, people take them for granted. A battery stores energy until we need it. When connected, the battery's chemical energy becomes electric energy. Electricity is powerful, and its uses are diverse, including ringing a doorbell, lighting a bulb, or running a motor.

We live in a plugged-in generation asking for lighter-weight, smaller, and more powerful batteries. Some people choose a smartphone based on a longer battery life. Society uses renewable energy more and more. Solar power is collected when the sun is shinning. Wind power is stored when the wind is blowing. Both solar and wind energy can be stored in batteries. There is a continual request for engineers to develop better batteries.

Electrical engineers solve problems involving electrical equipment. They design and test everything electrical, such as small electronic devices and large computer networks. Along with computer science engineers, they sometimes develop computers. They could work on a team to develop an electric car. Some electrical engineers design the systems that deliver electricity to your home. One thing is certain, as more and more of our everyday life is powered by electricity, electrical engineers will become more important.

Engineering in Your Everyday Life

Energy and Power Challenges

Electricity is the flow of electrons from one atom to another. Electrons spin in orbits around the nucleus, made of protons and neutrons. Picture a row of atoms with an electron leapfrogging from one atom to the next. The electron is negatively charged. When an electron leaves an atom, that atom becomes positively charged. When an extra electron is added to an atom, that atom

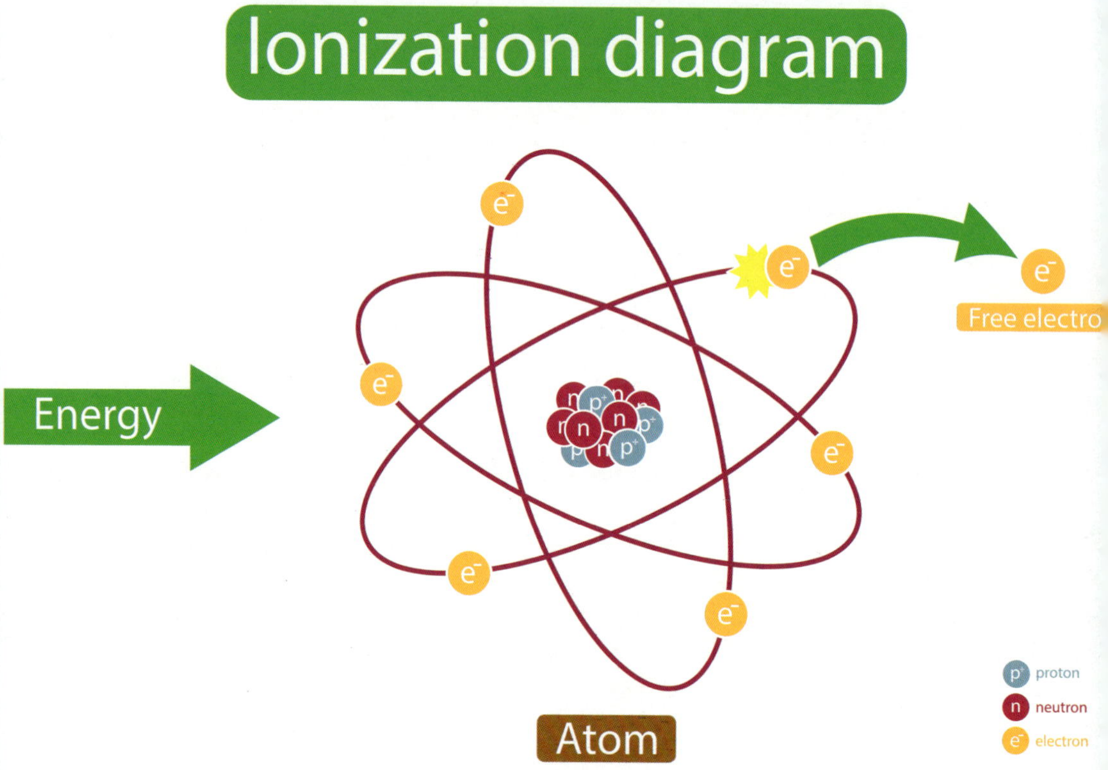

Ionization diagram

Energy → Atom → Free electron

p⁺ proton
n neutron
e⁻ electron

When energy is added to an atom, one electron can escape. This is known as a free electron. The flow of free electrons makes electricity possible.

24

becomes negatively charged. Atoms with a negative or positive charge are called ions.[1]

Electric current on the atomic level is measured by the number of electrons flowing past a given point every second. If you could see on an atomic level, you could measure current by counting the electrons that jumped onto and off of an atom over a second.[2] Current is measured in amperes.

How Batteries Work

Batteries convert chemical energy to electrical energy. In a battery, the electrons flow from one type of metal to a different type of metal. Between the two types of metal is usually a fluid with ions called an electrolyte.

Alessandro Volta (1745–1827), an eighteenth-century Italian electrical scientist, found that if he used a piece of paper soaked in salt water between silver and zinc plates, it produced an electrical current. The salt water acted as an electrolyte. To produce a larger current, Volta stacked many sets of silver, paper, and zinc and called his invention a voltaic pile.[3]

Pick up a AA, AAA, C, or D battery and look for 1.5V printed on it. The V stands for voltage, named after Volta. A battery's voltage is the strength of the battery, or the amount of electrons

Fully charged, these batteries will deliver 1.5 volts. The electrons flow out from the positive end and return to the negative end.

25

Engineering in Your Everyday Life

Drones

A drone is an unmanned aerial vehicle (UAV), which means no people are onboard.[4] A drone can fly into situations too dangerous for humans. The military uses a fixed wing drone that flies like an airplane. A second type of drone is the rotary drone that hovers like a helicopter.[5] A hovering drone can take aerial photographs. Most rotary drones operate on battery power.

it will push.[6] A voltmeter or multimeter will measure the voltage between two points.

Electricity in a Circuit

A circuit is the path where electrons flow. Electrons leave the battery's positive (+) terminal, flow around a circuit, and return to the battery's negative (−) terminal. Look at a battery and find the plus (+) and minus (−) symbols. Have you ever put a battery in backward to discover the electronic device does not work until the battery was flipped? Now you understand why.

Common 1.5 V batteries in AA, AAA, C, or D sizes are often made of carbon and zinc. Rechargeable batteries may be nickel-metal hydride (NiMH). Button-shaped batteries, such as those used for watches and hearing aids, often contain lithium (Li). In the following activity, you can use two coins as the two metals to make a voltaic pile battery similar to Volta's. A penny minted today is primarily zinc but coated with copper. A nickel is mostly copper but coated in nickel.[7]

Activity: Build a Penny–Nickel Battery

Nickels and pennies provide the plates of copper and zinc, respectively, to create a flow of electrons.

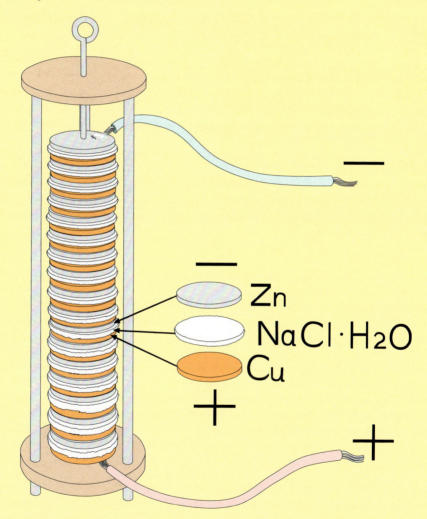

A voltaic pile has repeating layers of zinc (Zn), paper soaked in salt water (NaCl H$_2$O), and copper (Cu). The more layers of zinc (or pennies) and copper (or nickels), the higher the voltage.

Engineering in Your Everyday Life

Things You Will Need:

- **paper (cardstock, chipboard, or a pocket folder)**
- **12 pennies**
- **a pencil**
- **scissors**
- **goggles, for eye protection**
- **a glass**
- **water**
- **vinegar (any kind)**
- **salt**
- **paper towels**
- **12 nickels**
- **a multimeter**

■ **1.** Make twelve circles of paper by tracing around a penny and cut them out. Drop the paper circles in a glass. Put on your goggles. Pour water in the glass to cover the paper circles. Stir in a spoonful of vinegar and a spoonful of salt to make an electrolyte solution. Leave the paper circles to soak for about five minutes.

■ **2.** On a paper towel, lay out the twelve nickels in a row. Set a wet paper circle on each nickel. The paper should be soaking wet, but not dripping. Set a penny on top of each paper circle.

■ **3.** To make a voltaic stack, put each stack on top of the other. Check to see that the stack has the repeating pattern: nickel-paper-penny, nickel-paper-penny.

■ **4.** Use a voltmeter, or multimeter, to measure the voltage between the bottom nickel and the top penny. Try changing the number of coins to see the change in voltage.

Cars

Chapter 4

The power of a car comes from a machine, a motor. A motor takes energy and converts it to movement. In a car, that movement is the spinning of the wheels, propelling the car forward. Lawn mowers, mopeds, garage door openers, ceiling fans, and vacuum cleaners all move because of a motor. Many use electricity to convert energy to movement, but some, such as cars, trucks, motorcycles, and buses, primarily use internal combustion engines.

Mechanical engineers learn about stress and materials, mechanics and design. Mechanical engineers often make up the largest group in an engineering department. They work in a diverse number of industries, every group that works with power producing machines. Oil and gas development, chemical and manufacturing facilities, and power generation plants all need mechanical engineers.

Combustion Engines

Any car that runs on gasoline has an internal combustion engine where a controlled explosion provides the power. Hydrocarbon combustion is a chemical reaction where hydrocarbon (molecules with a mixture of hydrogen and carbon [HC]) reacts with oxygen (O_2) when ignited by a spark or extreme heat that produces water (H_2O) and carbon dioxide (CO_2) as products plus heat. The heat, or energy, is transformed into power in an engine.[1]

$$HC + O_2 \longrightarrow H_2O + CO_2 + heat$$

Fossil fuels are oil, natural gas, and coal. Over millions of years the fossil remains of ancient organisms, including dinosaurs, are

Engineering in Your Everyday Life

put under heat and pressure. They are converted into fossil fuels, which are loaded with chemical energy.

Have you heard of a car engine being referred to as a V6 or a V8? The number designates how many cylinders the engine block contains. Each cylinder has a piston that travels in only two directions, up and down. The piston turns the crankshaft, which turns the wheels. Each cylinder on a four-cycle, or four-stroke, engine goes through thousands of cycles to accelerate the car. The four cycles include intake, compression, combustion, and exhaust.

During cycle 1 (intake), the piston travels down, pulling in the fuel and air (containing oxygen) through the open intake valve. In cycle 2 (compression), the intake valve closes and the piston moves up, compressing or squeezing the fuel and air mixture. During cycle 3 (combustion), the spark plug sparks, igniting the combustion explosion, which pushes the piston down. The piston is connected to the crankshaft that transfers the power to the rest of the car, including the wheel axle. In cycle 4 (exhaust), the exhaust valve opens and the piston pushes the exhaust out the valve toward the muffler. Then the four cycles repeat.

Electric Cars

Electric cars have several advantages over the traditional internal combustion engine. The primary advantage is the lack of exhaust and resulting environmental impact. An electric vehicle is not emissions-free, however. That's because the electricity used to power the vehicle is usually produced in a way that causes emissions. It is a step in the direction of being more environmentally friendly. Many electric power plants burn natural gas, and some still burn coal. Both of these types of facilities produce emissions in the production

Cars

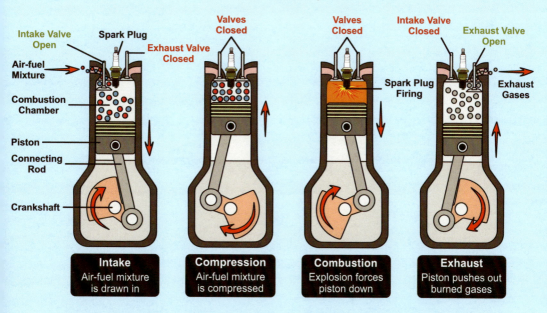

In a four-cycle (four-stroke) engine, the piston travels up and down to power the car.

of electricity. As technology advances, more electricity will be made with renewable resources, such as wind and solar.

A combustion engine has a battery that powers the engine starter, headlights, radio, and windshield wipers. In an electric vehicle, the battery is much more powerful because it provides the power to turn the tires. When the battery is plugged into a special wall socket, it is recharged.

One of the interesting things that electric cars do to be more efficient is to turn off when stopped even for a short time, for example at a red light. Another energy-efficient feature is that

Engineering in Your Everyday Life

Some homes and offices have electric-car charging stations, and more are being installed. Engineers are working to design car batteries that recharge faster, in less than an hour.

when the electric vehicle brakes, the battery recovers some of kinetic energy, recharging the battery.[2] A car traveling has kinetic energy. When the brake is applied, that energy is captured when the induction motor acts as a generator and the power generated is returned to the rechargeable battery.

Self-Driving Cars

The development of self-driving cars, or autonomous vehicles, is employing engineers in the fields of mechanical, electrical, and computer science. Self-driving cars utilize new technology, such as sensors, artificial intelligence, and machine learning. The light detection and ranging (LiDAR) sensor works with lasers to visually scan surroundings. Special wheel sensors measure each rotation to confirm the vehicle's location. Radar sensors detect and measure the speed of other cars in all directions. Police use a similar radar speed gun to determine speed of objects and for speed enforcement. Then all these sensors send information to the computer using artificial intelligence and machine learning to calculate the best direction and speed.[3]

To understand an electric car, you need to understand electromagnetism. There are two types of magnets, permanent magnets and electromagnets.[4] Examples of permanent magnets are bar, horseshoe, and refrigerator magnets. Permanent magnets do not need currents. Electromagnets are pieces of metal, containing iron, that have wires wound around them. When the electricity flows through the wires, the metal becomes magnetized as an electromagnet.

Activity: Small Motor Magic

The tip ends of the wire need to be within about an 1/8 inch (3.1 mm) of the magnets. Remove and adjust the wire until it whirls when placed on the magnet.

Cars

Things You Will Need:

- wire cutters
- at least 6 inches (15 cm) of bare copper wire
- pliers
- 3 neodymium magnets
- AA battery

■ **1.** Cut the copper wire to 6 inches (15 cm). Using the pliers, bend the wire into the shape of a heart. Do not connect the bottom of the heart.

■ **2.** Stack the three magnets. Balance the battery on top of the magnets with the negative end touching the top magnet. Balance the wire on top of the battery's positive end. Adjust the shape of the wire so that it only touches the top of the battery. The ends of the wire should extend past the battery into the magnetic field, but not touch the magnets.
The wire should start spinning![5]

■ **3.** If the wire is not spinning, there are several steps to check. Try turning the magnets upside down and reattach them to the battery. The magnets produce a magnetic field, but it is weaker when farther away from the magnets. The tips of the wire should be close enough to the magnet to be moved by the magnetic force. So, if the wire is not spinning, bend the wire so the tips are closer to the magnets. If the tips of the wire are too close, they will touch the magnet and spark. If the wire is too bowed, and the tips do not come below the battery, then the tips are not close enough to the magnets for the magnetic field to make an impact.

Smartphones

How often do you use a smartphone? They have changed our everyday lives. People used to leave messages on landline answering machines; now your call can go directly to the person you are calling, even when they are not at home. Smartphones also allow us to have access to the internet wherever we are located. A global positioning system (GPS) gives you information on how to get to destinations.

Engineers are challenged when developing new smartphones to include new features, but without making them larger, heavier, or too expensive. A more powerful lightweight battery means that the phone can go longer between charging. A larger memory allows the user to store more music and pictures. The technology is quickly developing with competing companies adding new features to their latest models every year. Many engineers contribute to these designs, including electrical engineers, computer scientists, and mechanical engineers.

How Does a Cell Phone Work?

A series of events happens between saying hello and it reaching your friend's smartphone. Your voice travels as sound waves. The sound waves enter the phone's microphone, where the sound is converted to electronic signals. The phone converts the waves into a code, a pattern of 1s and 0s. This happens on the circuit board inside the phone. The signal is then converted to radio waves and transmitted out the phone's antenna. Early cell phones

Smartphones

White vertical antennas on a cell phone tower face all directions to receive and transmit the radio signals.

Engineering in Your Everyday Life

had an antenna that poked out of the phone. Today the antenna is internal, but it is still there.

Invisible radio signals travel through the air to a cell phone tower's antenna.[1] Look for these towers in your neighborhood. They are tall metal towers, typically with several white rectangular antennas encircling the top. A cell tower sends a signal to a switching center. The switching center will then send the radio signal to whatever cell phone tower is closest to your friend. Sometimes the signal has to go through several towers before getting to its final destination.

Once your radio signal reaches your friend's phone, it now has to go through the this process in reverse to become sound. The signal enters through the antenna; the circuit board converts the radio wave signal to a code of 1s and 0s. Then the code is converted to sound. FInally, a speaker projects the sound. All that happens so quickly, it is amazing how often it works so well. When it does not work, sometimes it is because you do not have cell phone coverage. There are many causes, including not being close enough to a cell phone tower. Each tower sends and receives signals over an area of land. Many cell phone towers can handle a maximum number of 530 calls simultaneously.[2]

Inside a Smartphone

Think of a smartphone as a very small computer. It has a circuit board and a battery like a computer.[3] Cell phones have morphed into smartphones with many computer features. At the same time, computers have changed to have features of smartphones, including video conferencing capacity. The subscriber identity module (SIM card) identifies the phone for a particular cell number. A smartphone also has the software to communicate with

Smartphones

The blue circuit board borders three sides of the cell phone screen to carry signals from the buttons, camera, and speaker to the brains of the phone, the microprocessor.

a global positioning system (GPS) through special radio signals from satellites in outerspace.[4]

On a smartphone's circuit board, there are many transistors. They are so small that their diameter is twenty-five nanometers.[5] Human hair is approximately fifty thousand nanometers in diameter. Also on that circuit board is a semiconductor chip. The memory card stores your music, contacts, and photographs.

So what features do engineers work on when developing the next year's smartphone? The challenge is to make a smartphone

Engineering in Your Everyday Life

Sunshine to Electricity

Nuclear fusion on the sun produces a tremendous amount of renewable energy that can be captured as solar power. Solar cells are made of many little semiconductors, similar to those used in computer circuit boards. Semiconductors can conduct electricity, but not as well as metals.[6] The solar cell semiconductor absorbs a particular sunlight wavelength and then converts the sunlight to electricity. Several solar cells are connected together to make a solar panel.[7] The more panels that are connected, the more power it can produce. The cost of solar panels continues to decrease, making it a power solution for our homes and eventually our transportation.

that is minimum weight, minimum size, maximum memory, attractive, and still at the price point where the consumer will buy it. All this and new critical features, including the camera, continue to be improved.

Activity: Build an On and Off Button

Build a button that completes the circuit and lights the bulb when you push it.

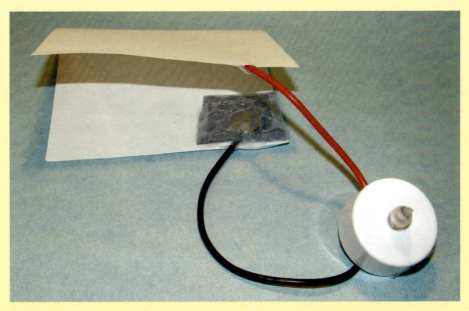

Red and black insulated 22-gauge copper electrical wires are used in this project. Ask for electrical wire at the hardware store.

Things You Will Need:

- a battery-operated tea light
- a small screwdriver (slot or Phillips depending on the tea light)
- red and black electrical wire, 6 inches (15 cm)
- needle-nose pliers
- an index card
- clear tape
- bubble wrap, 2 square inches (5 cm)

Engineering in Your Everyday Life

■ **1.** Turn on the tea light to check that the bulb works. Unscrew the back and remove the battery. Find the plus sign (+) for the positive side of the battery.

■ **2.** Look inside the tea light to locate the two wires that were in contact with the battery.

■ **3.** Pull apart the bonded red and black 6-inch (15-cm) wires.

■ **4.** Fold the index card in half. Tape the black wire to the negative side of the battery. Make a loop of tape and place it inside the index card. Put the negative side of the battery on the tape.

■ **5.** Connect the other end of the same wire to the tea light's negative wire, squeezing the connection with needle-nose pliers.

■ **6.** Cut a hole the size of the battery in the bubble wrap. Tape it around but not covering the battery. (The black square beneath the bubble wrap in the photo is just so the bubble wrap is easier to see.)

■ **7.** Connect the red wire to the tea light's positive wire.

■ **8.** Tape the other end of the red wire inside the index card so that when pressed closed, the red wire contacts the positive battery side.

■ **9.** Push the index card closed. Does this complete the circuit and turn on the light?

Robots

Unlike in the movies, most robots do not look at all like humans. A human-type robot is still an interesting design challenge because it could use our tools and work in our homes, schools, and offices. To walk similarly to a human, robots need pistons to work like muscles and a gyroscope to balance.[1] Most robots have sensors that allow them to take in information from around them. The robot's computer runs software to compute its given function. In this way, a robot can move and impact the world around it.[2]

Scientists, engineers, technicians, and others work on teams to design or improve robots. Robotics is designing, building, operating, and testing robots.[3] Mechanical, electrical, and computer science engineers are often good candidates to specialize in robotics. Robotics includes debugging programs, which is reading through and testing a robot's software if it is not working correctly. When the robot is working, it still needs routine calibrating and servicing by robotics technicians.[4]

What Can Robots Do?

Robots are being designed to do more and more for humans. Here are some examples where the time and energy into designing them has given humans great rewards.

Industrial robots make up about 90 percent of all working robots. These industrial robots do repetitive tasks with great accuracy in assembly lines. They are in factories where they build, paint, and weld cars and trucks.[5] At a metal foundry, robots work in environments where metal is melted, poured into molds, and

Engineering in Your Everyday Life

removed when cooled. Robots can also perform grinding and sanding on metal products.

There are two common kinds of industrial robots at work in factories: the SCARA and the articulated. A Selective Compliant Assembly Robot Arm (SCARA) has two joints that mimick a human arm's shoulder and elbow. The articulated robot has joints that are able to rotate. The ability to rotate means an articulated robot can turn a drill, tighten a screw, and move things in a circular fashion.[6]

Robots can also do mundane repetitive tasks that free humans up to do other things. For example, a home vacuum robot has sensors to allow it to "see" walls as well as an algorithm program that gives it the logic to cover an irregularly shaped room and the ability to respond to changes in flooring. For example, the vacuum robot can change suction on the carpet versus a flat surface.

Prosthetic Arms and Legs

Prosthetics allow a person the ability to pick up objects and walk, or even run. Doctors and biomedical engineers work to make the replacement limb function as closely to a natural limb as possible. A recent breakthrough is targeted muscle regeneration where a user can move their prosthetic just by thinking about it. For example, in a prosthetic foot, medical surgeons connect the nerve in the leg to the sensors for the prosthetic. The user thinks to move the foot and the sensors send a signal to the electric motor causing the movement.[7]

Robots

Animatronic robots act as pets or friends, with animation to make them resemble a human or animal. These sensors respond to humans with eyes that see with digital cameras and sensors that respond to touch.[8]

Would you want a dental student to practice on your teeth? Probably not, but the good news is that robots are being made for medical doctors, nurses, and dental students to practice on

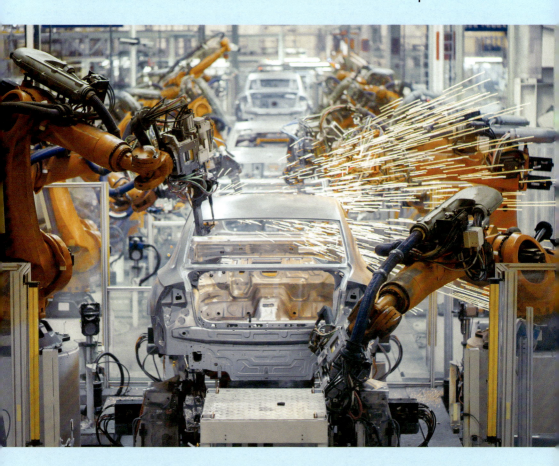

Sparks fly as these orange articulated robot arms work tirelessly with speedy precision to grind, drill, and build on the automobile assembly line.

Engineering in Your Everyday Life

instead of humans. These robot patients can simulate a heart attack and even deliver a robot baby.[9]

Police officers working with bombs benefit tremendously by sending a robot in to disarm a dangerous explosive. These are not just remote control machines. The robots take in information and calculate the response before taking action.[10]

Not unlike how the police force uses robots for dangerous situations, the military has many uses for robots to enter situations too hazardous for humans. The military is also utilizing robots to carry heavy loads and follow soldiers on foot for situations where a vehicle could not drive over the terrain.[11] A robot soldier that walks like a human is still in the developmental phase.

The National Oceanic and Atmospheric Administration (NOAA) deploys robots to explore the ocean floor. Water pressure limits how deep a scuba diver can travel. Think of the weight of the water squeezing the diver. Some robots travel 2 miles (3.2 kilometers) or more below the ocean surface. With three-fourths of the world covered in water, there are many coral reef and deep-sea discoveries ahead.[12]

Space exploration is another area where robots can solve many problems for humans. Robots can work without oxygen in temperatures where humans cannot. Robot arms helped build the International Space Station. Both the US Space Shuttle and International Space Station have large robotic arms.[13]

Activity: Build a Robot Arm

Build a robot arm, based on the SCARA model, that works off water pressure control.

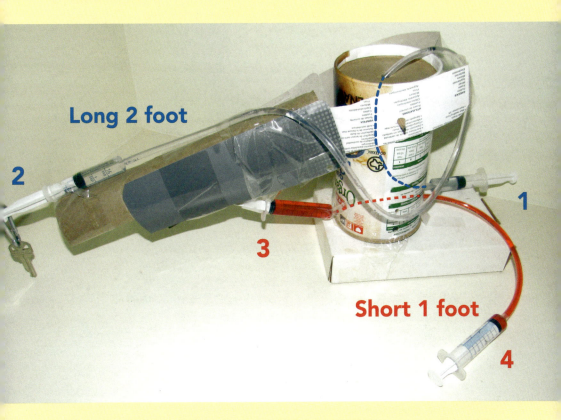

Pushing syringe #1 extends the plunger on syringe #2. The longer tubing between syringe #1 and #2 is laced through the oatmeal container. Pressing the syringe #4 plunger moves syringe #3 and the arm up.

Engineering in Your Everyday Life

Things You Will Need:

- **clear rubber tubing ¼ inch wide (6.3 mm), 3 feet (90 cm) long**
- **an empty oatmeal container or cardboard cylinder**
- **a hole punch**
- **a sharpened pencil**
- **2 rectangular cardboard boxes**
- **clear packing tape**
- **a paper towel tube**
- **4 oral syringes**
- **a funnel**
- **water**
- **food coloring (optional)**

■ **1.** Cut the tubing to make a 2-foot (60-cm) and a 1-foot (30-cm) piece.

■ **2.** On the oatmeal container, punch two holes opposite each other about 1 inch (2.5 cm) from the top.

■ **3.** Lace the shorter piece of tubing through the holes.

■ **4.** Punch a hole in the center of the bottom of the oatmeal container and another hole about 2 inches (5 cm) from the top. Lace the longer tubing through these two holes.

■ **5.** Punch two holes in the oatmeal container, opposite each other about 1 inch (2.5 cm) from the bottom. Push a pencil in one hole and out the other. The pencil is the arm axle.

■ **6.** Tape the oatmeal container, upside down, onto a cardboard box. Cut the second box to make two arm supports about 10 inches (25 cm) by 3 inches (7 cm). Punch a hole in each

48

Robots

and fit them over the pencil. Tape a paper towel tube between the arm supports.

■ **7.** Remove the four syringe plungers. Attach the syringes to each tube opening.

■ **8.** Place the robot in a sink to catch leaks. With help from a partner, pour water through the funnel into the longer tubing syringe (#1). When water drains from the lower syringe (#2), put in the plungers. Add a drop of red food coloring to the shorter tubing. Repeat the steps to fill and cap the second tubing.

■ **9.** Under the robotic arm, tape a syringe (#3) at an angle so it pushes as the plunger extends.

■ **10.** Tape syringe #1 to the cylinder base and syringe #2 at the arm end.

■ **11.** Test your robotic arm. Will it raise and lower? Will it pick up lightweight objects with a loop at the top?

Water

Water seems to be so abundant. It is one of the most common substances on the planet. Yet scientists are still unraveling the complexities of Earth's water system. About 98 percent of Earth's water is salt water, leaving only 2 percent fresh water.[1] Fresh water in rivers, lakes, and aquifers is sometimes too polluted for human consumption. Finding fresh water is a crisis for many people. We cannot live on salt water. Unless seaweed is a part of your diet, then the food you eat was grown with fresh water. Tomatoes are 95 percent water.[2]

Environmental engineers use engineering principles to keep air, water, and land clean and the people, plants, and animals that use it healthy. One of the focuses is developing solutions for clean water. Solutions can include minimizing waste-causing pollution. Engineers design systems to filter and treat waste disposal water. Another approach is to reduce the use of fresh water by individuals, farmers, and industries. Improved recycling decreases solid waste being dumped into water or seeping from landfills. The need for environmental engineers is expected to continue to increase, especially due to water projects.[3]

Why Is Having Enough Water a Concern?

Currently, the world population is pushing eight billion. Approximately eighty-three million people are added to the world population every year.[4] In the United States, most people use 50 to 80 gallons (189 to 303 liters) of water daily. Environmental

Water

engineers invent systems to reduce the use of fresh water in our homes, industries, and agriculture.

In some developing countries, people use only 5 gallons (19 L) a day.[5] Many need access to clean, fresh water. Much of the fresh water is trapped in aquifers, underground lakes flowing in the cracks and spaces between boulders and sand. These aquifers are tapped into by drilling water wells, some shallow and some a mile (1.6 km) or more deep. This is a real challenge for those who do not have access to electricity, pumps, or drilling equipment.

Turning Salt Water into Fresh Water

Desalination is the removal of salt from ocean water. Engineers use two primary approaches to remove the dissolved salts. One is

Florida Watershed

To control flooding in Florida, the shallow, bending Kissimmee River was replaced by a straight, deep canal. At the time, it was not understood how the river allowed the water to ever so slowly flood and flow through the everglades habitat. This seasonal flooding is an important part of the annual life cycle for the plants and animals. The shallow water where many birds walk to eat disappeared, and then the birds did also. Scientists discovered the importance of Florida watersheds, areas that funnel rainfall to rivers.[6] There is a major project to restore the Florida peninsula watersheds and the native vegetation and wildlife.[7]

Engineering in Your Everyday Life

done by boiling salt water, collecting the steam, and condensing it to water. This is repeated several times, with each water product becoming purer. The technical term is distillation. The second desalination process is called reverse osmosis, in which the seawater is pumped through a semipermeable membrane. The water pressure pushes the water molecules through the membrane and the salt and contaminates do not pass through. Both of these processes—distillation and reverse osmosis—use expensive equipment and lots of energy. Engineers continue to develop more cost effective processes to convert salt water to fresh water. New, more efficient processes produce more gallons worldwide every year. All the same, desalination might only be a solution for populations that live near an ocean. The cost of desalination water is two to three times that of the average water cost in the United States at $5 for 1000 gallons (3,785 L).[8]

Wastewater Treatment

Where does the water that leaves your home via the sewer go? Commonly, the sewer drains with the rainwater runoff to a local wastewater treatment facility. The water flows through screens with mesh in decreasing size to remove trash, leaves, and other debris. Typically, the water is mixed with air to speed the organic waste breakdown. This is called aeration. Next, the water will flow to settling ponds where, with a very slow flow rate, any material heavier than water will settle to the bottom. The product is then taken off the top. Skimmers similar to large sponges may float on the water to trap any particles lighter than water, such as oil. At this point, the water is ready to be chlorinated to kill any bacteria or germs. The water is tested for a number of things by a chemistry lab, including the pH, to be certain it is safe for wildlife. The water is often released to a local stream, river, or lake.

Water

Rows of water basins aerate sewage at this wastewater treatment facility. The air injected into the water is seen as ripples and bubbles on the surface.

Water in our homes comes from a water treatment plant. The plant will pump water from either a groundwater aquifer or local reservoir. The water is filtered, chlorinated, and tested by a chemistry lab before being pumped to users.

Activity: Test Water Faucet Aerators

Reduce your water use by half, maybe more. Get an adult's help on this experiment.

Faucet aerators reduce water use by mixing air with the water flow. The wire mesh separates the one water stream into many tiny streams with air between each stream.

Water

Things You Will Need:

- pliers
- 2 water-saving aerators
- 2 measuring cups
- a large bowl
- a stopwatch or phone with stopwatch function

■ **1.** Remove a sink faucet aerator using pliers, turning counterclockwise. Take the aerator to the hardware store.

■ **2.** If your faucet does not have an aerator, find the threads, which are spiral ridges like on the inside of a bottle cap, for an aerator. If the threads are on the inside, buy a male aerator. If the threads are on the outside, buy a female aerator. Measure the end of the faucet. Typical faucet diameters are regular (quarter diameter) 15/16" (23.8 mm), or junior (nickel diameter) 13/16" (20.6 mm).

■ **3.** At the hardware store, buy two aerators to fit your faucet with reduced water flow and extreme reduced water flow.

■ **4.** Make a table for the results. On each aerator, take three tests and an average.

■ **5.** Set a measuring cup under the faucet without an aerator. Put the second measuring cup and bowl within easy reach. Turn the water faucet to maximum flow and start the stopwatch. When the first measuring cup fills, slip the second cup under the flow. Pour the first cup in the bowl. Repeat. At ten seconds, remove the measuring cup and shut off the water. Record the water volume.

Engineering in Your Everyday Life

■ **6.** Repeat step 5 two times.

■ **7.** Turning clockwise by hand, add a reduced water aerator. Repeat steps 5 and 6.

■ **8.** Remove the water saving aerator. Install the extreme reduced water aerator. Repeat steps 5 and 6.

	Test 1 (cups or liters)	Test 2 (cups or liters)	Test 3 (cups or liters)	Average (cups or liters)
No aerator				
Reduced water flow aerator				
Extreme reduced water flow aerator				
Water savings				

Chapter Notes

Introduction
1. "Comparing the Engineering Design Process and the Scientific Method," Science Buddies, https://www.sciencebuddies.org/science-fair-projects/engineering-design-process/engineering-design-compare-scientific-method (accessed September 13, 2018).

■ Chapter 1
Bridges
1. Ryan Williams, "Types of Bridges," Bridge Physics, http://bridgephysics.weebly.com/types-of-bridges.html (accessed September 13, 2018).
2. Victor Labate, "Roman Engineering," Ancient History Encyclopedia, March 1, 2016, https://www.ancient.eu/Roman_Engineering/.
3. Dani Sneed, *The Man Who Invented the Ferris Wheel: The Genius of George Ferris* (Berkeley Heights, NJ: Enslow Publishers, 2014), pp. 7, 12.
4. John M. Venner, "HowStuffWorks Videos Understanding Tacoma Narrows Bridge," YouTube, October 2, 2012, https://www.youtube.com/watch?v=meLrQnuDc6o.

■ Chapter 2
Plastics
1. Cynthia Washam, "Plastics Go Green," *ChemMatters*, April 2010, p. 10, https://www.acs.org/content/dam/acsorg/education/resources/highschool/chemmatters/videos/chemmatters-april2010-bioplastics.pdf.
2. Andrea Rivera, *Plastic* (Minneapolis, MN: Abdo Zoom, 2018), p. 4.
3. Rivera, p. 11.
4. Liza Wallach Kloski and Nick Kloski, *Getting Started with 3D Printing* (San Francisco, CA: Maker Media, 2016), p. xi.
5. Lydia Sloan Cline, *3D Printing with Autodesk123D, Tinkercad, and MakerBot* (New York, NY: McGraw Hill Education, 2015), p. 5.
6. American Chemistry Council, "The History of Plastics Recycling," Plastics Make It Possible, updated November 2, 2017, https://www.plasticsmakeitpossible.com/about-plastics/history-of-plastics/the-history-of-recycling-plastic/.

Engineering in Your Everyday Life

7. Elise Moser, *What Milly Did: The Remarkable Pioneer of Plastics Recycling* (Toronto, CA: Groundwood Books, 2016), p. 16.
8. "Plastic Material Melt and Mould Temperatures," *Plastikcity*, https://www.plastikcity.co.uk/useful-stuff/material-melt-mould-temperatures (accessed September 15, 2018).
9. Moser, p. 39.
10. Moser, p. 45.
11. Bridget Heos, *Follow That Bottle!: A Plastic Recycling Journey* (Mankato, MN: Amicus Publishing, 2017), p. 5.
12. Washam, p. 10.
13. Steven Otfinoski, *Recycling and Upcycling: Science, Technology, Engineering* (New York, NY: Children's Press, 2016), p. 55.
14. Delaney Sulliman, "Making Bioplastics," Stanford University, http://stanford.edu/~dsull/Making_Bioplastics.pdf (accessed November 30, 2018).
15. Washam, p. 10.

Chapter 3
Batteries

1. Michael Geisen, *The Complete Middle School Study Guide: Everything You Need to Ace Science in One Big Fat Notebook* (New York, NY: Workman Publishing, 2016), pp. 159-160.
2. Geisen, p. 163.
3. Victoria G. Christensen, *How Batteries Work* (Minneapolis, MN: Lerner Publications, 2017), p. 11.
4. Lauren Newman, *Drones* (Ann Arbor, MI: Cherry Lake Publishing, 2018), p. 4.
5. Elsie Olson, *Drones* (Minneapolis, MN: Abdo Publishing, 2018), p. 16.
6. Chris Oxlade, *Using Batteries* (Chicago, IL: Heinemann Library, 2012), p. 14.
7. "Coin Production," United States Mint, updated on July 25, 2018, https://www.usmint.gov/learn/history/coin-production.

Chapter 4
Cars

1. Michael Geisen, *Everything You Need to Ace Science in One Big Fat Notebook* (New York, NY: Workman Publishing, 2016), p. 176.
2. "How Do Battery Electric Cars Work?" Union of Concerned Scientists, updated March 12, 2018, https://www.ucsusa.org/clean-vehicles/electric-vehicles/how-do-battery-electric-cars-work#.W7Pb0i3MxUM.
3. Christine Zuchora-Walske, *Self-Driving Cars* (Minneapolis, MN: ABDO, 2018), p. 27.

Chapter Notes

4. L.E. Carmichael, *Hybrid and Electric Vehicles* (Minneapolis, MN: ABDO, 2013), pp. 43-44.
5. Angie Smibert, *Mind-Blowing Physical Science Activities* (North Mankato, MN: Capstone Press, 2018), p.19.

Chapter 5
Smartphones

1. Nadia Higgins, *How Cell Phones Work* (Mankato, MN: The Child's World, 2012), p. 16.
2. Higgins, p. 17.
3. Richard Hantula, *How Do Cell Phones Work?* (New York, NY: Chelsea Clubhouse, 2010), pp. 18-19.
4. Hantula, *How Do Cell Phones Work?*, p. 22.
5. Michele Sequeira and Michael Westphal, *Cell Phone Science: What Happens When You Call and Why* (Albuquerque, NM: University of New Mexico Press, 2010), p. 59.
6. Richard Hantula, *Solar Power* (New York, NY: Chelsea Clubhouse, 2010), p. 17.
7. Hantula, *Solar Power*, p. 18.

Chapter 6
Robots

1. Rick Allen Leider, *Robots: Explore the World of Robots and How They Work for Us* (New York, NY: Sky Pony Press, 2015), p. 11.
2. Kathy Ceceri, *Robotics: Discover the Science and Technology of the Future* (White River Junction, VT: Nomad Press, 2012), pp. 6-7.
3. Ceceri, p. 2.
4. "How to Become a Robotics Engineer in 5 Steps," Learn.org, https://learn.org/articles/Robotics_Engineering_Become_a_Robotics_Engineer_in_5_Steps.html (accessed October 10, 2018).
5. Leider, p. 6.
6. Leider, pp. 22-23.
7. *National Geographic Science of Everything* (Washington, DC: National Geographic Society, 2013), p. 370.
8. Ceceri, p. 17.
9. Ceceri, pp. 24-25.
10. Leider, pp. 30-31.
11. Leider, pp. 26-27.
12. Leider, pp. 38-39.
13. Leider, p. 33.

Engineering in Your Everyday Life

■ Chapter 7
Water

1. Ellen Labrecque, *Clean Water* (Ann Arbor, MI: Cherry Lake, 2018), p. 4.
2. Melvin Berger, *All About Water* (New York, NY: Scholastic, 1993), p. 25.
3. "What Is an Environmental Engineer?" *Environmental Science*, https://www.environmentalscience.org/career/environmental-engineer (accessed October 10, 2018).
4. "World Population Projected to Reach 9.8 Billion, and 11.2 Billion in 2100," United Nations Department of Economic and Social Affairs, June 21, 2017, https://www.un.org/development/desa/en/news/population/world-population-prospects-2017.html.
5. Labrecque, p. 21.
6. "Watersheds," USDA Natural Resources Conservation Service, https://www.nrcs.usda.gov/wps/portal/nrcs/main/fl/water/watersheds/ (accessed October 2, 2018).
7. "Environmental Education Teacher's Guide: The Journey of Wayne Drop to the Everglades," US Corps of Engineers, Jacksonville District, http://141.232.10.32/education/educ_docs/teachers_guide/TeachersGuide.pdf (accessed November 30, 2018).
8. "Desalination and Water Recycling," Water for All, http://12.000.scripts.mit.edu/mission2017/desalination-and-water-recycling/ (accessed November 30, 2018).

bioplastic A plastic made using a biological substance, such as plants, instead of a petroleum substance, such as gasoline.

chemical energy The potential energy stored inside of an atom that holds it together.

combustion A chemical reaction where a fuel substance reacts with oxygen to produce heat and often light.

electromagnet A piece of metal, containing iron, with an insulated wire wound around it such that when a current flows through the wire, the metal becomes magnetized. When magnetized, the metal coiled in the wire gives off a magnetic field.

force A push or pull on an object that changes its movement, measured in joules or newton-meters.

generator A machine that changes mechanical energy, or motion, into electrical energy by spinning a loop of wire in a magnetic field.

motor A machine that changes electric energy into mechanical energy.

polymerization A chemical reaction where molecules, including carbon, link together in a repeating pattern to make long molecules.

power A measure of force times distance over a set time, measured in watts.

radio wave An electromagnetic wave with a wavelength within the range used for radio, but also television, cell phones, and other wireless communication.

renewable resource A supply that can be used again and again, such as solar, wind, biomass, tidal, and geothermal energy.

voltage A difference in electric potential energy between two points in an electric circuit, measured in volts.

weight A measure of gravitational pull times mass, measured in pounds or newtons.

Books

Furgang, Kathy. *21st Century Bridges*. New York, NY: Enslow Publishing, 2018.

Gardner, Robert, and Joshua Conklin. *Experiments for Future Engineers*. New York, NY: Enslow Publishing, 2018.

Labrecque, Ellen. *Clean Water*. Ann Arbor, MI: Cherry Lake Publishing, 2018.

McManus, Sean. *How to Code in 10 Easy Lessons*. Lake Forest, CA: Walter Foster Jr., 2015.

Newman, Lauren. *Drones*. Ann Arbor, MI: Cherry Lake Publishing, 2018.

Zuchora-Walske, Christine. *Self-Driving Cars*. Minneapolis, MN: Abdo Publishing, 2018.

Websites

Exploratorium: Engineering and Tinkering
www.exploratorium.edu/explore/engineering-tinkering
Find interesting activities, videos, and articles that help explain the engineering all around us.

Sandia Labs' Additive Manufacturing Program
www.youtube.com/watch?v=YCEr3FzSr_M
Click on Sandia Labs' world-class 3D printing program to watch cutting-edge technology design.

Science Buddies
www.sciencebuddies.org
Check out a variety of experiments on Science Buddies for science fair projects.

Index

A

activities
    build an on and off button, 41–42
    build a penny-nickel battery, 27–28
    build a robot arm, 47–49
    make biodegradable plastics, 21–22
    small motor magic, 34–35
    test bridge designs, 13–14
    test water faucet aerators, 54–56
aeration, 52
antennas, 36–38
aquifer, 51, 53
arch bridges, 10

B

batteries, 23–28
beam bridges, 8
biodegradable plastics, 20
bioplastics, 20
bridges, 8–14

C

cars, 29–35
cell phone towers, 37–38

chemical energy, 23, 25, 30
circuit, 26
circuit board, 39
combustion, 29–31
combustion engines, 29–30
compression, 9–10
cylinders, 30

D

desalination, 51–52
distillation, 52
drones, 26

E

electric cars, 30–33
electricity, 24–25
electrolytes, 25
electromagnet, 33
electrons, 24–25
engineering method, 6, 7

F

Ferris wheels, 11
fossil fuels, 30

G

global positioning system (GPS), 36, 39
groundwater, 53

63

Engineering in Your Everyday Life

I

International Space Station, 46
ions, 25

K

keystone, 10
kinetic energy, 32

N

NOAA, 46

O

osmosis, 52

P

pH, 52
plastics, 15–22
    bioplastics, 20
    chemical composition, 15
    manufacturing of, 15–17
    recycling, 17–19
poyhydroxyalkanoate (PHA), 20
polylactide acid (PLA), 20, 21

R

radio signals, 36–38
recycling, 17–19
reservoir, 53
robots, 43–49
Romans, 10

S

safety, 7

SCARA, 44
scientific method, 6, 7
self-driving cars, 33
smartphones, 36–42
Society of the Plastics Industry, 18
software, 7, 38, 43, 44
solar power, 40
sound waves, 36
SPI Coding System, 18
suspension bridges, 10

T

tension, 9–10
3D printing, 17
truss bridges, 9

V

Volta, Alessandro, 25
voltage, 25–28

W

wastewater treatment, 52–53
water, 50–56
watershed, 51